EMPIRE OF EDEN
Tom Laichas

Tom Laichas got his start in the 1980s, thanks to poet Peter Levitt's workshops and the late Helen Friedland's *Poetry/LA*. For three decades, Laichas taught history at Crossroads School in Santa Monica, California, meanwhile earning a Ph.D. (UCLA), and co-founding the journal *World History Connected* (University of Illinois Press). Since leaving the classroom to write full time, Laichas's work has appeared in *Ambit, High Window Review, Masque & Spectacle, Underfoot* and elsewhere. Tom Laichas lives with his wife Donna in Los Angeles. *Empire of Eden* is his first collection.

Empire of Eden

Tom Laichas

The High Window

First published in the UK in 2019 by The High Window Press
3 Grovely Close
Peatmoor
Swindon
SN5 5SN
Email: abbeygatebooks@yahoo.co.uk

The right of Tom Laichas to be identified as the author of this work has been
asserted by him in accordance with Copyright, Designs and Patent Act, 1988.
© Tom Laichas 2019
ISBN: 978-1-913201-14-2

Designed and typeset in Goudy Old Style
by The High Window Press.
Cover art: The Garden of Eden by Erastus Salisbury Field, ca. 1860. Museum of
Fine Arts, Boston. Image from Wikimedia Commons. Design by Taylor Barnes.
Printed and bound by Lulu.com.

CONTENTS

IV INTO THE WORLD

V   THE MURDERER AND HIS FAMILY

VI   THE OLD COUPLE

For Donna and Ari

and in memory of my parents Jim and Celia
my sister Janet and her husband Charles

And the Lord God
formed from the earth
every beast of the field
and every fowl of the heavens
He brought each to man to see what he
would call it

Whatever the man called each living thing
that was its name

Genesis 2:19

Are we a child or a name?

Fanny Howe

The Wait Won't Be Long

Sometimes, in boisterous play, the two children scuff the Garden's soil, exposing floorboards and joists. Sometimes, on a wander through the woods, they happen on paths too straight to be creature-made.

All day, the great tree shadows their questions. It sprouts from the center of a vast circumference. Its branches hang low with heavy fruit. Its height rockets toward a noontime zenith. Light as papier-mâché, it lofts well beyond sight.

Timber and starlight, sugar and clay: how long can such a confection last?

Lock children away in a room with a cake. Before closing the door, tell them no, don't eat a crumb.

Walk away.

The wait won't be long.

I

Beginning

B'resheet – Beginning

The Voice says: *B'resheet.*

The boy, cursed at birth with knowledge of speech, hears that word and knows, as sure as he breathes, that he's entered the story. As sure as he breathes, he hears every verse that will follow: the naming of creatures, the doubling of self, the fruit, the flight, the murder. *B'resheet* is the promise of happiness and horror.

To make a start, the fruit must be eaten. There's no other way.

A single seed, planted on the tongue, will be enough to wind time's spring-loaded engine, enough to muscle plot forward toward purpose.

So when it's time to eat the fruit, he'll eat.

A brave hungry boy.

The Boy's Questions

1.

The boy asks:

Before I woke, what was I?

The Voice tells him:

A name. A mercy. A word of command.

The boy:

I don't remember any of that.

The Voice:

It was a dream.

The boy:

What do you mean by "dream"?

The Voice:

Give the creatures their names. Do it now. In the dream, it has already happened.

2.

The Voice says:

Name the beasts.

The boy says:

Sun orbits, sunrise to dusk
Stars turn, from first dark to last

Wind soughs, bush to bough
Water curls, rock to reed

I name them too.
Why don't they obey?

The Boy Learns His Own Name

Name the creatures, the Voice says.

This makes no sense to the boy. In the whole of the Garden,
there is just one name. The Voice is in all living things.

The Voice persists: *Name my creatures, boy.*

> The boy sees *that* and thinks: I am *not-that.*
> He names *not-that* Lion.
>
> The boy sees *that* and thinks: I am *not-that.*
> He names *not-that* Elephant.
>
> The boy sees *that* and thinks: I am *not-that.*
> He names *not-that* Mouse.

All day long, the boy carves *I* from the hardwood of *not-I.*

By the time the syrup drips from the bitten fruit
the boy knows all its sweet poison can teach.

Dominion

1.

New to the world, the animals listen for every fresh sound. Sap seeps from trunk to crown. Tidal salt crusts the crisp reeds. Grassland soil swells in the sunshine.

From such music, each beast fashions a name as long as the day and as long as the night, chanted in rhythm with all living things.

Each learns its own name: its howl, its odor, its scat, the shape of its footpad on the new clay soil.

2.

Who can resist the little master? Armed to the teeth with tongue, he hurls names like arrows, never missing his mark. Pelt, scale and snout: by the end of the day, they're all nailed to the tree of his knowledge.

3.

The first songs silenced, the Voice revises the verse:

In the beginning, there was prose.

Left Hand

When the boy does his naming
he stretches out his right hand, palm down.

He says: *With my right hand I name you.*

This is because he remembers
a burning right hand
pressed to his own chest
commanding his lungs to begin their beat

inhale

exhale

inhale

exhale

About his left hand, the boy says nothing.

He won't name his weakness aloud.

Reborn

To name an animal, the boy's eyes must drill into the eyes of another. So many creatures, born to their otherness, avoid the boy's gaze.

The boy has a trick. He closes his eyes as if dreaming. An animal, restless, examines his lids, sniffing his odor.

At that moment, the boy's eyes snap open. He names the beast, fixing its purpose to his own.

This goes on all day. The animals, dazed, are reborn to the boy's service.

It is good, says the boy.

The creatures, denied voices, are shamed into croaks, trills, and clucks.

Named and Nameless

In the midst of the naming, the boy asks:

What's your name?

The Voice remembers that years in the future, others will ask this question. Then as now the voice replies:

I am what I am.

The boy:

That's not an answer. We're all what we are, nameless or no.

The Voice:

But it's you who must come when called.

The Boy Names the Dead

On his first naked day in the world, the boy fingers the earth's
unfurrowed soil. Nails and fingertips come up red. The little
master's name for this is *blood*.

Curious now (*why does the earth bleed?*), the boy's soft hands
dig deep into the garden's flesh. A finger's length down, he
finds skin and fascia, hard as tree bark. The boy knows that
this buried body, without movement or breath, was once a
living creature. Should he give it a name?

Finding a sharp stick, he digs deep for the corpse, freeing its
kneecap and rib. The skull is thick. The jaw recedes. The
bone is salted with sediment.

By day's end, he can see the whole of the mud-stained body.
He thinks hard for this creature's right name, but nothing
comes.

The boy asks: *If I am not first, what am I?*

The Voice does not reply.

Instead, sleep overcomes the boy. While he dreams, a blade
cuts his question from memory.

Awakened and refreshed, the boy remembers nothing. At his
feet, the soil lies flat and undisturbed. The boy wanders off,
back to naming birds.

Meanwhile, below ground, a mineral slurry ingests the ancient
body's muscle and infuses its bones.

Beneath this newly petrified skeleton lies another and, under
that, still another.

Down and down the layers go: mammalian, reptilian,
amphibian, pelagic.

Buried beneath the boy's feet are a thousand other Gardens, all of them burned in earlier Judgments.

Best that the boy know nothing of this.

Best he believe that he's first, born without sin into a new world.

Poisons

When the boy calls the beasts to his side, some proudly show him their venoms: toad's toxic skin, scorpion's barbed tail, spider's dull green spittle. The animals are innocent, but their venoms glisten with predatory greed.

Sensing the will at the heart of each poison, the boy treats each as a living creature, naming all, ensouling all.

Dripping with name, animate with purpose, the venoms patiently wait.

They know the garden will burn. They know that one brother will turn on another. They know that murder is best done in secret.

II

The Lie

Multitudes

The boy watches.

From the canopy, a percussive cloud lifts high, pulsing towards the south.

At boy-height, a swarm of smoke and hum hovers on the bank.

Within the white streamfall, a thousand thousand opalescent bodies leap against the rocks.

The boy's eyes move back and forth, from particular to plenitude. *Is starling one or many? Is locust more like a leaf or like a tree? Is salmon more like a single stone or a pebbled streambed?*

Names expand, names contract, like breath itself, drawn in, released.

The work is harder than he thought.

Cloud Forest

One morning, the boy walks beyond the Garden's bounds.
Outside the northern hedge, steep slopes rise.

The scents of resin and of rain draw the boy up and up.
Morning diffuses in thick vapor. The boy's hair goes wet and
lank. He's never heard such vegetable stillness. Unable to see
ahead, he moves into the mountain by touch and smell.

He's well above his Garden now, trespassing into greenery
reserved for living things unfit for lowland heat.

Creatures and trees keep themselves just out of his sight.
Night heron, Hyrcanian tiger, golden jackal. Velvet maple,
sweet chestnut, oriental beech.

The boy demands the mountains show themselves, but none
appear. For now, the uplands live in liberty.

Roots, rustling beneath the boy's two feet, feel his feral
weight.

They know there's little time left.

First Dog

First dog is small and mute, a garden-ready breed. No need to hunt: first dog lives on fruit and grass. No need to bark: there are no strangers here.

First dog nuzzles against the child's leg. The child rubs his spine. The child scratches his underjaw. When the child gives him a name, first dog's tail can't stop wagging.

Sit! Fetch! Heel!

First dog thinks each command is another name. He's rich with names! He spares no thought for wild creatures. He loves the child most of all.

First dog's near-kin find all this revolting. Coyote, Dingo, Jackal, Dhole, Fox and Wolf can't stand the smell of first dog's scat. If they sniff his piss on a rock or bush, they spray their own piss right over it.

Submissive to a child's command, first dog shames them all.

Raindrop

The boy looks into his first raindrop, a crystal hemisphere balanced on a leaf. The drop magnifies a brown cyst, its rounded armature raised from the leaf like a blister. Beneath, the suffering leaf leaks white sap.

The boy asks:

> What is this thing? All tortoise shell: no head, no limbs. Is it animal? Should I name it?

With his nail, he crushes the object into the leaf. It bleeds crimson.

The first murder is exactly this small. So small, the Voice says nothing about it. So small, the boy asks no forgiveness. So small, the verses forget it ever happened.

Later, the children eat the sweet fruit. Later, the garden burns to its roots. Later, brother murders brother.

No wonder. What, anyway, is murder?

Years before he has to ask, the boy, his fingernail stained, already knows.

The Lie

Says the Voice:

Name them all.

Says the boy:

I have named them.

The boy lies.

He can't hold his breath long enough to find all the fish skating the river's bottom. He squints at the high-soaring birds, their small silhouettes suspended on thermals. His slow-moving slippery fingers catch none of the worms whose last hind inches slip into soil.

At first, the lie shames the boy. And yet his pride swells:

I can keep secrets.

The lie pleases the boy.

Empire of Eden

Dominion's master, the boy has recited their names hour by
hour, teaching his tongue to recall each beast. Eel and
Elephant, Aphid and Ant, Muskrat and Mole, again and
again, every animal, every name, dawn to dusk.

Exhausted with effort, he closes his eyes and wanders in
dream.

> At the Edge of the Garden, all creatures rush to his side
> slithering, gliding, lumbering, swimming in hundreds, in
> thousands, trumpeting, howling.
>
> > Little Master!
> > Tell us our Names!
>
> He struggles to speak, remembering nothing. He rubs his eyes
> and scratches his scalp, but the names will not come.
>
> Into this silence, each creature screams. Beast-bodies writhe,
> then fall to pieces. Tendons unlace, joints disassemble, parts
> recombine.
>
> Here barking flowers, there braying flies. Wing fuses to tail. A
> horse-headed snail gallops from Eden on mucus and hoof.
>
> The name of creation is chaos.

The namer awakes, gasping for breath.

Slowly, he walks through the Garden by daylight. Slowly, he
loses his fear: everything is as it was.

Then, stabbing his chest, the dream's last sharp shard:

> What am I? What is adám?

After the Dream

The boy remembers his lie.

Now he knows: he must go on, name upon name.

There is no end to his work.

III

The Twinned Child

Didn't Ask for This

In the beginning, the Voice names the new creature *boy*.

Complete in itself, male and female, *boy* wanders the new world's wonders. If the child's gait is uncertain, if this new body founders, it isn't for longing.

The child stumbles again. So clumsy! Loneliness cripples the creature. The Voice will make for *boy* a companion.

The Voice flakes an obsidian core to a murderous edge, and slices the child from skullcap and sternum, through gonads and guts.

They slowly awaken: first *girl*, then *boy*. Shocked by their twoness, they throw themselves hard at each other. No matter how bruised their bodies, they can't break again into each other's bones.

why?

they ask

why?

Throughout the Garden, all beings whose bodies mingle female with male tremble in terror.

Snail and slug witness the violence. Sea star and sand dollar bury themselves in the beach sand. Sunflower's stigma and stamen shiver, sensing the knife's edge flicking through flesh.

This wound will never heal.

Hers & His

1.

Once torn apart, two freshly skinned bodies take the names given to them. The boy takes one name and the girl another.

Each learns the words *I* and *mine*.

It will be easy to swallow the fruit.

2.

The girl wonders aloud: *what name would I have chosen if the choice had been mine?*

3.

About his own name, the boy says nothing. He thinks: *it has been mine all along.*

He Names Her in Parts

The boy names the girl's body in parts as if each were a self-willed creature in need of a name's tight leash:

> Fingerjoints he names *fingerjoints.*
> wrists he names *wrists.*
> He names *elbow arm tit*
> then *shin knee cunt.*

> From top to bottom
> he names and he names.
> Then, in a stupor, he sleeps.

She laughs at him. While he dreams, she names his parts in turn:

> This part pig, that part goat
> dog of course and porcupine
> rat, whale, and cold slim fish

Then she too falls asleep.

> She dreams that sutures come loose
> that heads, torsos and limbs
> collapse in two heaps.

> She dreams of a Flood and a Boat.
> She dreams a forced march up a gangplank
> body parts brought aboard in a satchel.

> She dreams of rain's end.
> She dreams of a mountain.
> She dreams of the parts, spilled on the new shore.
> She dreams of two bodies remade into one.

> She dreams of a creature, lonesome and frightened but
> once again

> whole.

Climbing the Tree

The Voice says, *Don't eat the fruit.*

Not a word about climbing the tree.

The two children pull themselves up to the tree's lowest ledge, finding their footholds in the trunk's jagged wall. The girl stretches one leg, shifts weight to the other, extending a hand to steady her sibling.

Their muscles relax into effort. Gravity, fresh-made, forgives. In this way they climb.

So many creatures, unseen from the ground. The boy and the girl, now experienced namers, dispatch each with a flick of the tongue:

> *capuchin monkey* and *three-toed sloth*
> *loris* and *toucan*
> *bald-headed eagle*
> *indiri*
> *opossum*
> *malabar tree toad*

Reaching the canopy, the children recline on a meadow of leaf. Nothing obstructs the view. They gaze beyond hedge, beyond river, out to the world's salt waters.

There's no reason to fear. These children haven't yet picked the fruit. Death is still unchosen.

All afternoon a hawk soars below them. They tell one another:

> *We could jump from this height*

> *We could fly like that bird*

> *Our lives have no end*

> *We don't need wings*

Eggplant

At first, there are no eggs in Eden. All animals are virgins, neither carnal nor carnivorous.

So, on their first day together, the boy and girl cannot guess how to name the bulbous purple tumor bobbing from a stem amid lavender flowers and tumescent yellow stamens.

Because the children are hungry, they bite into its chitinous skin, chewing its bland pulp. Its hard seeds are big as ticks.

They spit and laugh, like they spat raw potato, yam and turnip.

Later, the Garden in ash, the boy and girl will go hungry. Poking broken sticks into embers, they'll find potato, yam and turnip, now softened and chewable.

Finally, they'll see the eggplant. They'll break through the charred skin and take small consoling bites of the creamy white flesh.

Without thinking, they'll know its name.

Eden is Another Name for Ithaca

Before the forbidden fruit ripens, before the first Troy rises, the boy builds a small skiff. Wind-blown, he makes his way from mountain scarp to shingled shore, along the entire inland sea.

He names the water creatures: urchin and worm, flying fish and diving gull, leaping dolphin and sideways crab.

Coasting past mangroved islands, he glimpses a nymph, an enchantress and a one-eyed giant. Knowing only one god, he treats the others with indifference. He names them and sails on.

At home, no drunken suitors brawl for his kingdom, no princeling son sharpens his sword, no loyal wife sits at her loom for ten thousand days weaving wool into wild excuses.

Untroubled by tide and story, the boy returns, unscarred and wholly unchanged.

At the Beach

The Garden's western edge slopes into ocean. None of the four-legged beasts linger there long.

The boy asks the girl:

> *Why go there? It's all dunes and green weed. It's the same on every beach. Walk with me by the river.*

She tells him:

> *This morning, the tide went out. I walked along the rocks. I saw creatures there, new creatures, wedged in crevices, buried in shingle.*
>
> *Come with me tonight – we can name them together! All day I thought of names. We can name them sand dollar or sand louse, urchin or grunion, limpet or lamprey, clam or crab – whatever we like.*
>
> *Swim with me past the waves and into the warm grey water. It's salty, the way your mouth tastes. It moves like our chests, beating again and again.*
>
> *I know it's alive.*
>
> *I named it Leviathan.*

Ravenous

Boy and girl live on melon and berry
    mango, pear, guava
    grape and plum.

Spat from their mouths, every pit and seed
    digs its own burrow
    sprouts, leafs, flowers and fruits.

And so they eat again
    he, half-asleep
    she, naming each syrup as it coats her tongue.

For these sweet juices
    they're ravenous
    hungry for every growing thing.

Even before that singular fruit
    these children
    want more.

High Place

The Voice never said that *garden* is the same thing as *world*.
So, from the garden's high place, the children stare east into
blue lands beyond the hedge.

Then they gasp in surprise.

There, in the haze, a city and its people.

Who are these strangers, bodies wrapped in animal skin? Why
do they pull a tethered calf, a calf who sweats with fear, a calf
who digs in its hooves, straining against every forward step?
Why do they force the animal down to the flat stone. Why do
they cut its throat and cheer its puddled blood?

The children see this and know.

Should they ever disobey, there will be no going back.

The Serpent

It swims in the girl's daylight when she looks at the sky: a floater in her eye's vitreous fluid. The night's tides carry the worm from horizon to horizon across the dark zenith.

She asks the boy. He sees it too.

One day, just as the luscious fruit comes into view, her left pupil grows big and hurricane black. A serpent burrows out, jaws agape. From the boy's eye, the same.

Later, they wonder how their desires could swim in their eyes for so long, seen but unseen.

Serpent Speaks

When Serpent promises the animals that he'll talk to the children, the other creatures urge him on. If shaped into sense, their caws, their coos and their caterwauls would say:

Tell them, Serpent! Make the little masters release my name to me. Tonight let me be free!

All afternoon, picnicking on the Garden's fruit, Serpent converses with boy and girl. From the edge of a thicket, the creatures listen. But Serpent says nothing of naming, nothing of animal souls and their theft. Instead, he speaks of Subtlety and Sapience, Cosmos and Creation.

Lies, all of it. How can he do this? That limbless worm!

In the end, the Garden burns. The innocent creatures flee this way and that. But, when the bawling children scream their names, every animal must obey. Braying and bleating, they follow the children east into sin.

That night, Mongoose and Eagle rip open Serpent's belly. They eat him alive.

Too late. From an ash-warmed nest, new serpents hatch by the hundreds.

They easily find their way out to the world.

The Fruit

The fruit needs no reptilian tongue to tempt the children.

Stemwise, it slithers into their dreams. *Taste me. Chew me. Swallow me up.* The sweet juice and pulp sluices down their sleeping throats.

The children awaken. They already know what it will mean to let this fruit into their mouths: labor and labor pains. Such suffering!

But also sweetness. Now and then, such sweetness.

They know what will come. Do you think they are stupid? Aren't they, both of them, prophets?

From the garden's high place, looking over the hedge, they've seen cities and villages. They've seen their savage gardenless neighbors. But, when the breeze is just right, it carries a sugared scent from every hovel and house.

The fruit is the only way out.

They eat.

The moment they swallow, the cosmos collapses in on their skins. They are one with no one else.

The dream said nothing about such sudden loneliness. Terrified, wholly estranged from the world, they shiver in clear winter air.

But the fruit keeps its promises, and its scent warms their bodies, its heat driving every slow thought from their brains. They burn together, the children: alone and together.

From a vast distance, the Voice speaks:

You shall surely die.

The Voice too keeps its promises.

The Hedge

Created before the newborns and their gated child-garden, before the villagers outside the fence, Other-man wanders grasslands.

Other-man smells the hedge closing up around the new-fashioned beasts and the two children.

Air closes in with the trees, stifling and hot. An odor of feral fear rises from the hemmed-in herds.

What do these children know? Set here, in the midst of this hardscape, all seems to them fresh-made and lovely.

Every name given the beasts is an iron stake hammered in rock, prisoning free creatures. These children: what do they know?

To make his escape, Other-man tunnels under the hedge. Then he hesitates. He loves beasts too well to leave them behind. He can't help them all. Maybe a few can be saved from this naming.

Heavy-muscled, heavy-browed, Other-man remains. Meanwhile, the children play with matches.

Other-man

Other-man, also kneaded from clay
    walks by himself
    full grown and awake.

Hair as thick as a bear's, brows heavy
    eyes brown, large as two moons
    better to see in the dark.

He knows no names, but he knows the creatures
    their ways and their hungers:
    by pawprint and piss he knows them.

If he wants their company, they walk with him willingly.
    He has a creaturely walk, light and lively.
    They lick his hand; he tickles their ears.

As for the boy, he's furtive, hiding himself
    behind trees, behind boulders.
    He's hiding from Other-man.

He thinks himself clever, the boy.
    But Other-man knows the boy's breathing
    his odors, his footfalls as loud as a shadow's.

Other-man watches the boy claim dominion
    over creatures who moments before
    had told their own stories free from this magic.

Split down the middle, the Voice twins the boy
    a knife making them male and female.
    Other-man remains undivided and whole.

On the Garden's last day, the animals follow the boy
    away from the flames and into the world,
    beyond Other-man's knowing.

Belonging to no one
        alone in the wasteland. Other-man runs
        this way and that, lost in the wreckage.

The Garden burns hot, a furnace.
        Other-man's bones crack, his marrow boils.
        His skull splits, his brain pan sizzles.

Or else he escapes, running wild with grief
        to the edge of a field.

Or else he is Cain's first kill.
        Some say that, too.

IV

Into the World

Look Back

The Garden burns. The children run from the smoldering hedge, stumbling on for hours. Bent double, they pause, gagging on rancid ash.

They can't stop here. Near-blind, they dumb-fumble further away. They're exhausted. Again, they halt, turn back, watch, weep, cough blood, turn ahead and run.

Again the children turn their faces back toward the burnt child-garden. Sobbing, they cough black slurry out of their chests. Again, crouching, they turn and run.

> Much later, a woman will flee from a burning city. She'll hear the same command: don't look back.
>
> She will stop for breath. One last look.
>
> That's all it will take for a dead sea to boil into her legs. Her blood will clot mineral-white. Her salt body will break at the waist, a road-rooted stump.

These children look back and live. The woman will look back and die. Where is the justice in that?

Think of it this way. The children run toward a country of salt. It will be salt for the rest of their lives.

The Meal

1.

When the garden burns, the animals run to the Karun. They leap into the river's mud, swimming its corpulent grease.

Seeing them scattered, the children call them to come.

Only Dog answers.

Cat hangs back, licks his singed paw, and counts cinders and stars.

2.

On the crown of a far hill, the children collapse into sleep. The next black morning, they wake.

They again call the creatures, each by its name. Obedient, the suffering animals gather, their fat and muscle still burning hot.

The children sniff the exposed meat of these animal wounds.

Hungry. These children are hungry.

Their food quickly learns: when called, do not come meekly.

All About Dog

Boy and girl, now husband and wife,
slaughter and eat their first kill.

No animal answers again to its name –
except Dog, who eats the portion set aside for him.

Late that night, Wolf catches Dog's nape in his teeth.

Wolf's foreleg shatters Dog's spine.
Wolf's jaw crushes Dog's windpipe.

Wolf says:

> *You're a damned traitor, obeying that boy.*
> *You think we forgot your true name?*

Orphaned

Creator gods make bad fathers and worse mothers. They plant the promise of death in the garden's core and dare their children to eat. They never forget a child's small lies. They never regret their own rage.

Full-grown into husband and wife, the Garden's twins make their way into the backlands. He becomes humanity's angry father. She, its resentful mother.

The fruit's first lesson: children deserve exactly what they get.

The Human Ways

Stumbling into the country out east, husband and wife become beggars. Their bellies are sunken and smooth, without birth-scars. They wear nothing but burnt leaves. They're not trusted.

Godborn, one crofter says. Another, fingering his scythe and eyeing the stained altar at the crossroads, spits and whispers: *They run from their god. If we take them in, it won't go well for us.*

Who can blame the second man? His own harsh gods teach him to burn beasts and babies for love of screams and sorrows.

Still, those who live outside the Garden remember another story's beginning:

> *Once, we were strangers.*

So the village takes them in, teaching them the human ways.

Their Own Children

Their own children need names.

The Voice, anger fading, gives them a name-list, incised into verse. Abel to Zebulon, Zipporah to Abishag: every good name is here.

Knowing how names foretell, the husband and wife ask the Voice:

> *Of these amulets, which will protect our daughters and sons against the world's evil?*

The Voice replies:

> *You think you can yoke them with names, as if they were oxen? They'll be just as you were: they'll pull hard to the left and hard to the right. They'll break your plow and trample your fields. All you can do is teach them and hope for the best.*
>
> *Think of it as another curse.*

In the Morning, She Tells Him

I had the strangest dream. You'd named the animals, all that
walk, crawl and slither.

In my dream, I named the rest, the silent rooted creatures:
    Seagrass, cat's tail, river-rush.
    Hemlock, oleander, nightcap.

In my dream you said:
    They're without souls, just green wands.

But husband: I've heard stalks of wheat shurrushing in the
wind. I've heard them sing!

    I told Cain.

    He hears the singing too.

V

The Murderer and his Family

The Elder Brother's Questions

Cain wonders how his brother can kill what their father has named. He wonders why a gift has to bleed before it burns.

He thinks about smoke.

Muscle, wool and bone do not burn clean. Why not the sweet smoke of straw and stubble? The stalks do not shriek when cut.

Why can't his brother see that? Why can't his father's god?

What is so hard for them to understand?

Cain Remembers the Word

Cain is shocked. He's never seen so much blood at once, spoiling the good ground.

Killing was his brother's way. Crouching just out of sight, Cain had watched the ram struggle and go limp, listening as the Voice praised his brother for the knife's sharp work.

Should he burn his brother's body, like his brother burned the ram?

There's a word Cain's wanting, a word that makes it right.

The word, he remembers, is *sacrifice*.

Neighbor

Cain is mistaken. The word is not sacrifice. It's murder. A fine distinction, but enough to force Cain to flee his father, to plug his ears against the Voice's anger. Enough to palsy Cain's right hand, the one that held the edged obsidian.

He runs eastward, to the peopled districts his parents glimpsed from Eden's hills. From a distance, strangers watch him walk their lands, his right hand balled up in a fist suspended from a puppet's limp arm.

His disfigurement is the mark of a god's intense regard.

They don't want him here, but they can't force him back.

The village men take him to the edge of their farmlands, to an empty mudbrick shack. They grab one of their daughters, dragging her to him. They give him land, seed, oxen and plough. They don't say a word to explain themselves.

Cain replies to their silence with silence. With his left hand, he plants emmer in the Spring. With his left hand, he holds the curved knife that cuts the sheaf.

Wordless, he takes the woman given to him.

Wordless, he harnesses oxen to plow.

Wordless, he raises daughters and sons.

Wordless, he grows old and older, dying every day of his life.

The Murderer's Son

Born of a mute father and a deaf mother
a scarred father and a thin-lipped mother
a father who can't explain
a mother inured to silence.

Like his father, he plants emmer with his left hand.

In his left hand, he holds the reaping hook.
Stooped over the ground, he cuts down the tall stalks.

His mother knows his father's secrets.
She hides them in a lockbox under her tongue.

The Murderer's Daughters

Everyone knows it takes seven generations to expiate sin:
seven fathers and seven sons.

So the townsfolk shun Cain's son as they shunned his father.
They'll shun the grandsons too, when it's time.

But the daughters: that's another matter.

The Murderer's Father

After the murder, Cain's father rages into the dark hills,
cursing creation, burning his first son's field to ash,
butchering the younger son's herd, leaving meat to the
maggots. He sobs, sleeps, wakes and walks on, his legs
stuttering beneath him.

After some days, a bundle slung at her chest, Cain's mother
comes after her husband along his trail of cinder and
slaughter.

He's there, on the massacred ground, shaking and weeping.

She stands before him, her hand on his cheek.

No time for that, she says.

She turns the bundle toward him.

*This is our son, our third boy. Take him in the crook of your
arm.*

Teach him the names.

Sing to him, like you sang for his brothers.

Home

1.

The husband, having lost two sons, returns home from his mad inconsolable grief. An infant still lives, a third boy. There will be more, both sons and daughters.

Anguish burrows within him, eating at his sleep. He names these dreamless nights *dishonor*.

Never again, he says. *Never again*. He decides: this new son and all of the children to come must obey his every word, must ask for every freedom.

His wife warns him:

> *If you push them hard, they will break.*

In silence he looks at the woman. He thinks:

> *She too must be made to obey.*

2.

The wife, what can she do? She lives among strangers. If she runs off, where would she go? She has no mother or father. Her childhood is ash.

She must stay and stay.

She feels a sickness rise her belly. She gives this nausea a name: it is *shame*.

The Murderer's Sisters

In another version, the husband and wife name only their sons. The daughters are nameless.

To name is to honor. That which is honored, owes. The debt must be paid. These unnamed daughters, granted no dignity, stand safe beyond arm's reach.

Their father knows the names of all living creatures, but does not know these daughters of his.

Their mother knows the price paid for taking a name from a husband. She keeps her daughters out of his sight, nameless as dim and untouchable stars.

The beasts know these daughters by scent. The beasts know their feral eyes, their stillness. They know these women by posture: alert, ready to fight or flee.

These sisters, silent in sunlight, keep to the fiction. In a house where brother kills brother, it is best to give and take names only in a new moon's blue shadow.

The beasts know this too.

The Lesson

The exiled wife takes her first daughter out to the field.

She grabs her daughter's head from behind and holds it tight so the girl can't look away.

Mamma, the girl says, *you're hurting me!*

It's time you learn! her mother says. *See that? That's what it's like!*

A dozen yards away, a couple of dogs are fucking. The act deforms both the sire and the bitch. His pelvis bends at right angles to his back; her hind legs splay under his weight.

The girl sobs and shakes.

Then, suddenly calmed, she asks softly:

Why do you stay with him?

The question surprises the woman. Her hands fall limp from her daughter's hot cheeks. Her chin trembles.

There was nobody else. And it was good at first. But he got selfish. He's a selfish son of a bitch.

For a long moment, there's silence between them. Then, from her daughter:

And you're different?

The wife's anger collapses in on itself. Her shoulders slump.

You're right. I'm not any different. It's the fruit. Shouldn't have eaten it. Those seeds – you can never shit them out.

VII

The Old Couple

Verse-haunted

Long before ink has claimed a single page, verses devour wife and husband. As they sleep, each sound of this lifelong song unfolds its looming letter-shape.

No matter how far they run, the hungry stories pursue them. Every night, the verses catch and consume them.

In dream, they foresee the whole future of their tribe: suffering inflicted, suffering endured.

Every day, the dream is true.

They're prophets, this wife and husband. Not that anyone listens. Not that listening matters. The verses can't be soothed, can't be resisted, can't be eluded.

Over long years, wife and husband learn to bear this affliction. They take slow breaths to quiet their agony. They imagine a day that is not night.

The Grandchildren

The grandchildren tell a simple story:

You sinned. We suffer.

It is because you sinned
that we suffer and endure squalor
that we suffer and endure deception
that we suffer and endure betrayal

It is because you sinned
that we suffer and endure lewdness
that we suffer and endure perjury
that we suffer and endure disrespect

It is because you sinned
that we suffer and endure impiety
that we suffer and endure impurity of speech
that we suffer and endure false denial

It is because you sinned
that we suffer and endure bribery
that we suffer and endure cynicism
that we suffer and endure evil gossip

It is because you sinned
that we suffer and endure fraud
that we suffer and endure gluttony
that we suffer and endure drunkenness

It is because you sinned
that we suffer and endure arrogance
that we suffer and endure tyranny
that we suffer and endure sideways glances

It is because you sinned
that we suffer and endure vanity
that we suffer and endure impudence
that we suffer and endure anarchy

It is because you sinned
that we suffer and endure scheming
that we suffer and endure conspiracy
that we suffer and endure selfish love

It is because you sinned
that we suffer and endure obduracy
that we suffer and endure murder
that we suffer and endure causeless hatred

It is because you sinned
that we suffer and endure pleasure in the pain of others
that we suffer and endure ignorance
that we suffer and endure rebelliousness

It is because you sinned
that we suffer and endure rape
that we suffer and endure robbery by night
that we suffer and endure manslaughter

It is because you sinned
that we suffer and endure adultery
that we suffer and endure oppression
that we suffer and endure lying

It is because you sinned
that we suffer and endure hypocrisy.
that we suffer and endure corruptions of the spirit
that we suffer and endure sickness of heart

You sinned. We suffer.

To these grandchildren, the old couple says:

Did we teach you any of these evils? Are you angry? Then
thump your fists against your own ribs. Hit them hard, until
they break.

Then go.

Long Lives

The first husband and wife bury their children, one after another. They bury their children, their grandchildren, their grandchildren's children.

Through their long lives, they die every death in the world. Their eyes see death. Their ears hear death. Their lungs inhale its odor. Their fingers lave death with oil and their arms bury the flesh of their flesh.

They live and they live and they live, this husband and wife. They beg for deaths of their own.

Of this crushing abasement, the verses say nothing.

That silence is mercy.

A Game at the River

From a distance, the old husband and wife watch the boy Noah,
who kneels at the river's edge, stripping the emmer and weaving its
leaves into a fist-wide coracle.

Once he's caulked the toy with acacia gum, he releases it into the
water. Seized by the current, the vessel spins toward the foam. Noah
runs alongside, fast on his legs, as the churn hurls the boat into
cataract.

Wife and husband see far downstream. As they watch, the boy's legs
lengthen, the little boat grows and the waters howl. Above the hot
plain, verses crowd into thunderheads.

Wife and husband know their time on earth is near its end. They
smell the storm ahead. There is nothing to be done.

You can't outrun a flood of verses. You let them carry you or else
you drown.

Fragrance

Husband and wife will die before the Flood. As their bodies fail, they sniff the dark breeze and exchange a glance. They look out on the world's murders and feel the Voice's anger swell.

They know what's coming. It's the fury of a parent who's lost a child.

They know the smell of a world that rage will drown.

And they know too that after every violence, children and flocks and grasses return in their numbers, as living things do.

If the Voice asked his advice, the old husband would give it:

Look.

The world you made isn't easy to kill.

Sin won't stay drowned. It will all happen again. There's no starting over.

Forget this deep storm of yours.

Instead, ask the dove to fetch herbs and laurel leaves. Inhale their fragrance.

This is how we saved ourselves.

One Day

All these years together. All these names: Girl and Boy, Wife and Husband, Mother and Father.

Living in squalor, Voice-forgotten: only these two truly understand one another.

Sometimes names are like sutures, binding the gash into a tight scar. Year after year, every old name calls to its other, each one half of a whole.

One day, the woman and man quietly gift one another new names.

No one else knows these names, not even the story.

The First Man Recites his Will

1

I named them all. Green names and flesh names. Scale names, feather names. Names humid and cold. Names that itched, names that hurt.

I can't remember a damn thing anymore. I watch creatures skitter, unafraid of my words. I'm too slow with their names to halt their hurry.

Years past, the verses moved on toward younger men's stories, the names of small kings, fathers and sons, sung in long lists, men building towers toward heaven.

The story's always the same. It's mine. But the story forgets my own name.

Those verses and I are the same: we've let our beginnings go dark.

2.

I have mourned the deaths of every beast I ever named.

I have stood at my children's graves, and at my grandchildren's.

I have said Kaddish a thousand thousand times.

Do not mark my grave.

Let me go out as I came, nameless.

Undo for me what I cannot undo for others.

The Return

Her story ends first. The widower carries her body west, into the ruined grove. He crosses the sump of a stream into an ashen meadow.

He has outlived his daughters and sons, his grandchildren and great-grandchildren. He has outlived clans, tribes and nations.

He has outlived his wife.

He will bury her here, within the old Garden, where a green hedge arched over a gate. Within that gate was a well-watered place, its delight now a slag-heap so blasted, the widower knows, that in all the ages to come, nothing good will grow here.

Now he feels the fruit's syrup losing its long power over his heart. From his sunken chest, beaten blood feels its way back into his limbs.

Once, the Voice said: *Never return*. Now he is here, and the Voice says nothing.

A small breeze cools his face.

He and she belong here. This is home.

Acknowledgements

I am grateful to the editors of journals in which earlier versions of these poems appeared. *Adelaide*: 'At the Edge of Air', 'Renamed', 'Other-man'; *Blue Unicorn*: 'Cloud Forest', 'The Human Ways', 'Possession'; *Convergence*: 'The Fruit'; *Eclectica*: 'Naming the Poisons', 'When the Garden Burns'; *High Window*: B'reshith', 'Didn't Ask for This', 'Name Them', 'Serpent Speaks'; *Lotus-eater*: 'First Dog', 'Left Hand'; *Panoply*: 'Ravenous'; *UnderfootPoetry*: 'The Hedge', 'Her Name', 'Home', 'Named and Nameless', 'Nocturnal Habits', 'One Day', 'Released', 'The Seasons', 'The World'.

I owe deep thanks to friends who read this work closely and shared their thoughtful responses: Virginia Benitez, Laurel Ann Bogen, Gabriel Botnik, Danah Ezekiel Clark, Peter Levitt, Freddy Nager, Mike Shaler, Zoey Zimmerman and, for her cover design, Taylor Barnes.

I am especially indebted to Susan Suntree and Deirdre Gainor, who gave much of their time to read and respond to successive drafts.

My deep appreciation as well to David Cooke at the High Window Press. His support and thoughtful counsel have made this work possible.

Above all, I am grateful to my daughter Ari and my wife Donna for their love and support, now and always.

.